DOG TREATS RECIPES
cookbook

Wallace Durante

COPYRIGHT

All rights reserved. No part of this publication may be reproduced, distributed, or transmitted in any form or by any means, including photocopying, recording, or other electronic or mechanical methods, without the prior written permission of the publisher, except in the case of brief quotations embodied in critical reviews and certain other non-commercial uses permitted by copyright law.

Copyright © Wallace Durante, 2024.

TABLE OF CONTENTS

Copyright   iii
Introduction   1

Chapter One: 3
BISCUITS AND COOKIES FOR CRUNCHY FUN

- Peanut Butter and Oat Balls   4
- Chicken and Rice Cookies   5
- Carrot and Parsley Biscuits   6
- Sweet Potato and Cinnamon Bites   7
- Pumpkin and Coconut Drops   8
- Beef and Cheese Twists   9
- Turkey and Quinoa Bars   10
- Spinach and Cheddar Balls   11
- Salmon and Potato Chews   12
- Peanut Butter and Pumpkin Cookies   13
- Zucchini and Chicken Bites   14
- Cheese and Oat Bars   15
- Turkey and Brown Rice Balls   16
- Beef and Carrot Patties   17
- Sweet Potato and Cheese Squares   18

- Lamb and Rice Meatballs — 19
- Cheddar and Bacon Biscuits — 20
- Tuna and Quinoa Balls — 21
- Cheese and Turkey Sticks — 22
- Chicken and Spinach Muffins — 23
- Beef and Pumpkin Jerky — 24

Chapter Two: 25
CAKES AND MUFFINS FOR SOFT AND MOIST TREATS

- Carrot Cake Pup cakes — 26
- Turkey and Cranberry Crunch Bars — 27
- Peanut Butter and Blueberry Bliss Bites — 28
- Blueberry and Banana Pup Muffins — 29
- Beef and Pumpkin Paw Print Cookies — 30
- Chicken and Berry Biscuit Delights — 31
- Turkey and Veggie Muffins — 32
- Cheesy Bacon Biscuit Bites — 33
- Turkey and Sweet Potato Slices — 34

Chapter Three: 35
FROZEN AND FROSTY TREATS FOR COOLING AND REFRESHING SNACKS

- Blueberry and Yogurt Frozen Pops — 36
- Apple and Banana Frosty Bites — 37
- Tuna and Pumpkin Paw-Sicles — 38
- Chicken Liver Delights — 39
- Sweet Potato and Turkey Wraps — 40

Chapter Four: 41
NO-BAKE AND EASY TREATS FOR QUICK AND SIMPLE SNACKS

- Chicken and Cheddar Chew Sticks   42
- Apple and Carrot Pupcakes   43
- Pumpkin Oat Cookies   44
- Liver Nibbles   45
- Coconut and Berry Bliss Bars   46
- Banana and Peanut Butter Swirls   47
- Pumpkin and Blueberry Bites   48
- Oatmeal and Apple Rounds   49
- Strawberry and Sweet Potato Cookies   50
- Cheesy Egg Bites   51
- Pumpkin and Egg Delights   52
- Blueberry Egg Muffins   53

Conclusion   54

Introduction

I discovered myself looking for homemade dog treat recipes as I set out on my mission to give my furry friends the love and care they deserve. These recipes needed to fit in seamlessly with my hectic schedule. Time seemed to fly by as I balanced a never-ending list of duties, longing for a means to make sure my four-legged pals received nutritious meals even when we were on the go.

That's when I got an idea, and I decided to compile a collection of delicious homemade dog treat recipes that-would satisfy both their dietary requirements and my time limits.

Each recipe in this "*Cookbook for busy Dog parents*" has been painstakingly created, assuring a harmonious balance of flavors and nutrients while giving busy people like me top priority.

I looked for materials that are readily available with an emphasis on simplicity so that I could quickly prepare these delicious treats without taking valuable time out of my busy schedule. You'll find yourself effortlessly preparing mouthwatering treats that will leave tails wagging and hearts brimming with joy.

Whether you're a busy professional, a parent juggling multiple responsibilities, or simply seeking to indulge your furry friends with wholesome treats, this cookbook is your ultimate companion.

Chapter One

BISCUITS AND COOKIES FOR CRUNCHY FUN

In this chapter, you find all the recipes that can be baked in the oven and have a crunchy or chewy texture. These are great for rewarding your dog, keeping their teeth clean, and satisfying their appetite.

1

PEANUT BUTTER AND OAT BALLS

 Preparation Time: 15 minutes
Cooking Time: No cooking required
Number of Servings: Approximately 20 balls

Ingredients

- 1 cup peanut butter (Rich in protein, healthy fats)
- 2 cups oats (High in fiber, vitamins, and minerals)

Instructions

- In a mixing bowl, combine the peanut butter and oats.
- Mix well until the ingredients are fully incorporated.
- Take small portions of the mixture and roll them into bite-sized balls.
- Place the balls on a baking sheet and refrigerate for about 1 hour to set.
- Once set, the peanut butter and oat balls are ready to be served to your furry friend.

2

CHICKEN AND RICE COOKIES

▶ Preparation Time: 20 minutes
Cooking Time: 15-20 minutes
Number of Servings: Approximately 30 cookies ◀

Ingredients

- 1 cup cooked chicken, shredded (Excellent source of protein)
- 1 cup cooked rice (Good source of carbohydrates)
- 1 cup flour

Instructions

- Preheat your oven to 350°F (175°C) and line a baking sheet with parchment paper.
- In a mixing bowl, combine the shredded chicken, cooked rice, and flour.
- Mix well until the ingredients are thoroughly combined and form a dough-like consistency.
- Roll out the dough on a lightly floured surface to about 1/4-inch thickness.
- Use cookie cutters to cut out desired shapes or simply cut the dough into small squares.
- Place the cookies on the prepared baking sheet and bake for 15-20 minutes, or until golden brown and crispy.
- Allow the cookies to cool completely before serving them to your dog.

CARROT AND PARSLEY BISCUITS

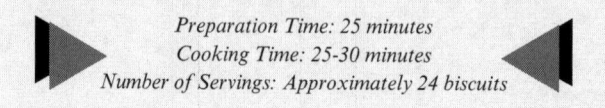

Preparation Time: 25 minutes
Cooking Time: 25-30 minutes
Number of Servings: Approximately 24 biscuits

Ingredients

- 2 cups grated carrots (High in beta-carotene, vitamins)
- 1/4 cup fresh parsley, chopped (Rich in vitamins K, C, A)
- 2 cups flour

Instructions

- Preheat your oven to 350°F (175°C) and line a baking sheet with parchment paper.
- In a mixing bowl, combine the grated carrots, chopped parsley, and flour.
- Mix well until all the ingredients are evenly distributed and form a dough.
- Roll out the dough on a lightly floured surface to about 1/4-inch thickness.
- Use cookie cutters to cut out desired shapes or simply cut the dough into small squares.
- Place the biscuits on the prepared baking sheet and bake for 25-30 minutes, or until firm and lightly browned.
- Allow the biscuits to cool completely before offering them to your furry companion.

4

SWEET POTATO AND CINNAMON BITES

Preparation Time: 15 minutes
Cooking Time: 20-25 minutes
Number of Servings: Approximately 25 bites

Ingredients
- 2 cups mashed sweet potatoes

Nutritional Value: High in fiber, vitamins, and minerals
- 1 teaspoon cinnamon

Nutritional Value: Antioxidant properties
- 2 cups flour

Instructions
- Preheat your oven to 350°F (175°C) and line a baking sheet with parchment paper.
- In a mixing bowl, combine the mashed sweet potatoes, cinnamon, and flour.
- Mix well until all the ingredients are thoroughly combined and form a dough.
- Roll out the dough on a lightly floured surface to about 1/4-inch thickness.
- Use a small cookie cutter or knife to cut out bite-sized shapes or simply cut the dough into small squares.
- Place the bites on the prepared baking sheet and bake for 20-25 minutes, or until firm.
- Once baked, let the sweet potato and cinnamon bites cool completely before serving them to your dog.

5

PUMPKIN AND COCONUT DROPS

 Preparation Time: 10 minutes
Cooking Time: 1 hour (refrigeration)
Number of Servings: Approximately 30 drops

Ingredients

- 1 cup pumpkin puree
  (Rich in fiber, vitamins A and C)
- 1 cup shredded coconut
  (Good source of healthy fats)

Instructions

- Line a baking sheet with parchment paper.
- In a mixing bowl, combine the pumpkin puree and shredded coconut.
- Stir well until the ingredients are thoroughly mixed.
- Drop small spoonfuls of the mixture onto the prepared baking sheet.
- Place the baking sheet in the refrigerator for about 1 hour, or until the drops are set.
- Once set, transfer the pumpkin and coconut drops to an airtight container and store them in the refrigerator.
- Offer these delicious drops to your furry friend as a tasty treat.

6

BEEF AND CHEESE TWISTS

Preparation Time: 20 minutes
Cooking Time: 15-20 minutes
Number of Servings: Approximately 15 twists

Ingredients

- 1 cup cooked ground beef (Excellent source of protein)
- 1 cup grated cheese (High in calcium and protein)

Instructions

- Preheat your oven to 350°F (175°C) and line a baking sheet with parchment paper.
- In a mixing bowl, combine the cooked ground beef and grated cheese.
- Mix well until the ingredients are thoroughly combined.
- Take a small portion of the mixture and roll it into a thin strip, resembling a twist.
- Place the twisted strips on the prepared baking sheet.
- Bake in the preheated oven for 15-20 minutes, or until firm and slightly crispy.
- Allow the beef and cheese twists to cool completely before offering them to your dog.

7

TURKEY AND QUINOA BARS

 Preparation Time: 25 minutes
Cooking Time: 25-30 minutes
Number of Servings: Approximately 20 bars

Ingredients

- 1 cup cooked ground turkey (Lean protein source)
- 1 cup cooked quinoa (Rich in protein, fiber, and minerals)
- 1 egg

Instructions

- Preheat your oven to 350°F (175°C) and grease a baking dish.
- In a mixing bowl, combine the cooked ground turkey, cooked quinoa, and egg.
- Mix well until all the ingredients are thoroughly combined.
- Transfer the mixture to the greased baking dish and spread it out evenly.
- Bake in the preheated oven for 25-30 minutes, or until the bars are firm and set.
- Once baked, allow the turkey and quinoa bars to cool completely before cutting them into small bars or squares.
- Store the bars in an airtight container in the refrigerator until ready to serve.

8

SPINACH AND CHEDDAR BALLS

 Preparation Time: 15 minutes
Cooking Time: 15-20 minutes
Number of Servings: Approximately 25 balls

Ingredients

- 2 cups fresh spinach leaves (High in iron, vitamins, and minerals)
- 1 cup grated cheddar cheese (Good source of calcium and protein)

Instructions

- Preheat your oven to 350°F (175°C) and line a baking sheet with parchment paper.
- In a food processor, blend the fresh spinach leaves until finely chopped.
- In a mixing bowl, combine the chopped spinach and grated cheddar cheese.
- Mix well until all the ingredients are evenly distributed and form a dough-like consistency.
- Take small portions of the mixture and roll them into bite-sized balls.
- Place the balls on the prepared baking sheet and bake for 15-20 minutes, or until firm and lightly browned.
- Allow the spinach and cheddar balls to cool completely before serving them to your furry companion.

SALMON AND POTATO CHEWS

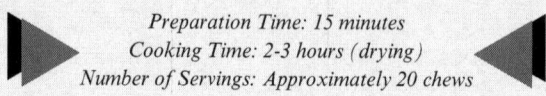

▶ *Preparation Time: 15 minutes*
Cooking Time: 2-3 hours (drying) ◀
Number of Servings: Approximately 20 chews

Ingredients
- 1 cup cooked salmon, flaked (Rich in omega-3 fatty acids)
- 1 cup mashed potatoes (Good source of carbohydrates)

Instructions
- Preheat your oven to 200°F (95°C) and line a baking sheet with parchment paper.
- In a mixing bowl, combine the cooked salmon and mashed potatoes.
- Mix well until the ingredients are thoroughly combined.
- Take small portions of the mixture and shape them into long chews or sticks.
- Place the chews on the prepared baking sheet.
- Bake in the preheated oven for 2-3 hours, or until the chews are dried and chewy.
- Once baked, allow the salmon and potato chews to cool completely before offering them to your dog.

10

PEANUT BUTTER AND PUMPKIN COOKIES

Preparation Time: 20 minutes
Cooking Time: 15-20 minutes
Number of Servings: Approximately 30 cookies

Ingredients

- 1 cup peanut butter (High in healthy fats and protein)
- 1 cup pumpkin puree (Rich in fiber, vitamins A and C)
- 2 cups oat flour (Whole grain with fiber)

Instructions

- Preheat your oven to 350°F (175°C) and line a baking sheet with parchment paper.
- In a mixing bowl, combine the peanut butter, pumpkin puree, and oat flour.
- Mix well until all the ingredients are thoroughly combined and form a cookie dough-like consistency.
- Roll out the dough on a lightly floured surface to about 1/4-inch thickness.
- Use cookie cutters to cut out desired shapes or simply cut the dough into small squares.
- Place the cookies on the prepared baking sheet and bake for 15-20 minutes, or until golden brown.
- Allow the peanut butter and pumpkin cookies to cool completely before serving them to your furry friend.

11

ZUCCHINI AND CHICKEN BITES

 Preparation Time: 25 minutes
Cooking Time: 20-25 minutes
Number of Servings: Approximately 25 bites

Ingredients
- 2 cups grated zucchini (Low-calorie vegetable with vitamins and minerals)
- 1 cup cooked chicken, shredded (Lean protein source)
- 2 cups flour (Carbohydrate base)

Instructions
- Preheat your oven to 350°F (175°C) and line a baking sheet with parchment paper.
- In a mixing bowl, combine the grated zucchini, shredded chicken, and flour.
- Mix well until all the ingredients are thoroughly combined and form a dough.
- Roll out the dough on a lightly floured surface to about 1/4-inch thickness.
- Use a small cookie cutter or knife to cut out bite-sized shapes or simply cut the dough into small squares.
- Place the bites on the prepared baking sheet and bake for 20-25 minutes, or until firm and lightly browned.
- Allow the zucchini and chicken bites to cool completely before serving them to your dog.

12

CHEESE AND OAT BARS

 Preparation Time: 20 minutes
Cooking Time: 25-30 minutes
Number of Servings: Approximately 20 bars

Ingredients

- 2 cups grated cheese (High in calcium and protein)
- 2 cups oats (Whole grain with fiber)
- 1 egg (Protein source)

Instructions

- Preheat your oven to 350°F (175°C) and grease a baking dish.
- In a mixing bowl, combine the grated cheese, oats, and egg.
- Mix well until all the ingredients are thoroughly combined.
- Transfer the mixture to the greased baking dish and spread it out evenly.
- Bake in the preheated oven for 25-30 minutes, or until the bars are firm and slightly golden.
- Once baked, allow the cheese and oat bars to cool completely before cutting them into small bars or squares.
- Store the bars in an airtight container in the refrigerator until ready to serve.

13

TURKEY AND BROWN RICE BALLS

Preparation Time: 15 minutes
Cooking Time: 15-20 minutes
Number of Servings: Approximately 25 balls

Ingredients

- 2 cups cooked ground turkey (Lean protein source)
- 1 cup cooked brown rice (Whole grain with fiber)

Instructions

- Preheat your oven to 350°F (175°C) and line a baking sheet with parchment paper.
- In a mixing bowl, combine the cooked ground turkey and cooked brown rice.
- Mix well until the ingredients are thoroughly combined.
- Take small portions of the mixture and roll them into bite-sized balls.
- Place the balls on the prepared baking sheet and bake for 15-20 minutes, or until firm and cooked through.
- Allow the turkey and brown rice balls to cool completely before serving them to your dog.

14

BEEF AND CARROT PATTIES

Preparation Time: 20 minutes
Cooking Time: 20-25 minutes
Number of Servings: Approximately 15 patties

Ingredients
- 1 cup cooked ground beef (Protein source)
- 1 cup grated carrots (Rich in vitamins and antioxidants)

Instructions
- Preheat your oven to 350°F (175°C) and line a baking sheet with parchment paper.
- In a mixing bowl, combine the cooked ground beef and grated carrots.
- Mix well until the ingredients are thoroughly combined.
- Take a portion of the mixture and shape it into a patty.
- Place the patties on the prepared baking sheet.
- Bake in the preheated oven for 20-25 minutes, or until the patties are cooked through.
- Once baked, allow the beef and carrot patties to cool completely before serving them to your furry friend.

15

SWEET POTATO AND CHEESE SQUARES

Preparation Time: 25 minutes
Cooking Time: 25-30 minutes
Number of Servings: Approximately 20 squares

Ingredients

- 2 cups mashed sweet potatoes (High in fiber, vitamins, and minerals)
- 1 cup grated cheese (Protein and calcium source)
- 2 cups flour (Carbohydrate base)

Instructions

- Preheat your oven to 350°F (175°C) and line a baking sheet with parchment paper.
- In a mixing bowl, combine the mashed sweet potatoes, grated cheese, and flour.
- Mix well until all the ingredients are thoroughly combined and form a dough.
- Roll out the dough on a lightly floured surface to about 1/4-inch thickness.
- Cut the dough into small squares using a knife or pizza cutter.
- Place the squares on the prepared baking sheet and bake for 25-30 minutes, or until firm and lightly golden.
- Allow the sweet potato and cheese squares to cool completely before offering them to your dog.

16

LAMB AND RICE MEATBALLS

Preparation Time: 15 minutes
Cooking Time: 15-20 minutes
Number of Servings: Approximately 20 meatballs

Ingredients

- 1 cup cooked ground lamb(Protein source)
- 1 cup cooked rice(Whole grain with fiber)

Instructions

- Preheat your oven to 350°F (175°C) and line a baking sheet with parchment paper.
- In a mixing bowl, combine the cooked ground lamb and cooked rice.
- Mix well until the ingredients are thoroughly combined.
- Take small portions of the mixture and roll them into meatballs.
- Place the meatballs on the prepared baking sheet and bake for 15-20 minutes, or until firm and cooked through.
- Allow the lamb and rice meatballs to cool completely before serving them to your dog.

CHEDDAR AND BACON BISCUITS

Preparation Time: 20 minutes
Cooking Time: 25-30 minutes
Number of Servings: Approximately 30 biscuits

Ingredients

- 2 cups grated cheddar cheese (Protein and calcium source)
- 1/2 cup cooked bacon, crumbled (Flavorful protein)
- 2 cups flour (Carbohydrate base)

Instructions

- Preheat your oven to 350°F (175°C) and line a baking sheet with parchment paper.
- In a mixing bowl, combine the grated cheddar cheese, crumbled bacon, and flour.
- Mix well until all the ingredients are evenly distributed and form a dough.
- Roll out the dough on a lightly floured surface to about 1/4-inch thickness.
- Use cookie cutters to cut out desired shapes or simply cut the dough into small squares.
- Place the biscuits on the prepared baking sheet and bake for 25-30 minutes, or until firm and lightly golden.
- Allow the cheddar and bacon biscuits to cool completely before offering them to your furry companion.

18

TUNA AND QUINOA BALLS

 Preparation Time: 15 minutes
Cooking Time: 15-20 minutes
Number of Servings: Approximately 25 balls

Ingredients

- 2 cans tuna in water, drained (Omega-3 fatty acids)
- 1 cup cooked quinoa (Protein and whole grain)
- 1 egg

Instructions

- Preheat your oven to 350°F (175°C) and line a baking sheet with parchment paper.
- In a mixing bowl, combine the drained tuna, cooked quinoa, and egg.
- Mix well until all the ingredients are thoroughly combined.
- Take small portions of the mixture and roll them into bite-sized balls.
- Place the balls on the prepared baking sheet and bake for 15-20 minutes, or until firm and cooked through.
- Allow the tuna and quinoa balls to cool completely before serving them to your dog.

19

CHICKEN AND SPINACH MUFFINS

Preparation Time: 15 minutes
Cooking Time: 25-30 minutes
Number of Servings: Approximately 12 muffins

Ingredients
- 2 cups cooked chicken, shredded (Lean protein)
- 2 cups fresh spinach leaves, chopped (Rich in vitamins and minerals)
- 2 cups flour Carbohydrate base)
- 1 cup chicken broth

Instructions
- Preheat your oven to 350°F (175°C) and line a muffin tin with paper liners.
- In a mixing bowl, combine the shredded chicken, chopped spinach, flour, and chicken broth.
- Mix well until all the ingredients are thoroughly combined and form a batter.
- Fill each muffin cup with the batter, about 3/4 full.
- Bake in the preheated oven for 25-30 minutes, or until the muffins are firm and lightly golden on top.
- Allow the chicken and spinach muffins to cool completely before serving them to your furry friend.

20

BEEF AND PUMPKIN JERKY

Preparation Time: 10 minutes
Cooking Time: 2-3 hours
Number of Servings: Varies (as it depends on thickness)

Ingredients

- 1 pound lean beef, thinly sliced (Protein source)
- 1 cup pumpkin puree (fiber and vitamins)

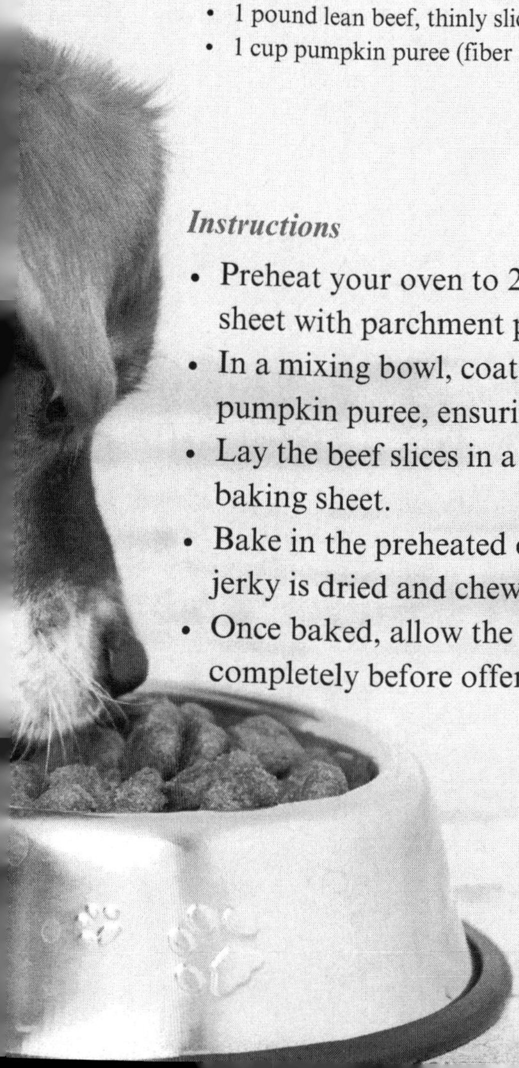

Instructions

- Preheat your oven to 200°F (95°C) and line a baking sheet with parchment paper.
- In a mixing bowl, coat the thinly sliced beef with pumpkin puree, ensuring it is evenly coated.
- Lay the beef slices in a single layer on the prepared baking sheet.
- Bake in the preheated oven for 2-3 hours, or until the jerky is dried and chewy.
- Once baked, allow the beef and pumpkin jerky to cool completely before offering it to your dog.

21

CHEESE AND TURKEY STICKS

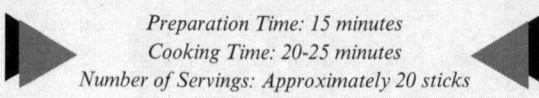

Preparation Time: 15 minutes
Cooking Time: 20-25 minutes
Number of Servings: Approximately 20 sticks

Ingredients

- 2 cups grated cheese (Calcium and protein source)
- 1 cup cooked turkey, diced (Lean protein)
- 2 cups flour (Carbohydrate base)
- 1/2 cup water

Instructions

- Preheat your oven to 350°F (175°C) and line a baking sheet with parchment paper.
- In a mixing bowl, combine the grated cheese, diced turkey, flour, and water.
- Mix well until all the ingredients are thoroughly combined and form a dough.
- Roll out the dough on a lightly floured surface to about 1/4-inch thickness.
- Cut the dough into long sticks, resembling sticks of cheese.
- Place the sticks on the prepared baking sheet and bake for 20-25 minutes, or until firm and lightly golden.
- Allow the cheese and turkey sticks to cool completely before serving them to your dog.

Chapter Two

CAKES AND MUFFINS FOR SOFT AND MOIST TREATS

This chapter contains all the recipes that are baked in muffin tins or cake pans and have a soft or moist texture. These are great for celebrating your dog's birthday, special occasions, or just as a treat.

CARROT CAKE PUP CAKES

 Preparation Time: 20 minutes
Cooking Time: 20-25 minutes
Number of Servings: 12 pupcakes

Ingredients

- 2 cups grated carrots (Rich in beta-carotene)
- 1/2 cup unsweetened applesauce (Natural sweetener)
- 1/3 cup coconut oil (Healthy fat)
- 1/4 cup honey (Natural sweetener)
- 2 eggs (Protein source)
- 1 teaspoon vanilla extract
- 2 cups whole wheat flour (Provides fiber)
- 1 teaspoon baking soda
- 1/2 teaspoon cinnamon (Adds flavor)
- A pinch of salt

Instructions

- Preheat your oven to 350°F (175°C) and line a muffin tin with paper liners.
- In a large bowl, mix grated carrots, applesauce, coconut oil, honey, eggs, and vanilla extract.
- In a separate bowl, whisk together the flour, baking soda, cinnamon, and salt.
- Combine the wet and dry ingredients until just mixed.
- Spoon the batter into muffin cups.
- Bake for 20-25 minutes or until a toothpick comes out clean.
- Allow pupcakes to cool before serving.

2

TURKEY & CRANBERRY CRUNCH BARS

 Preparation Time: 15 minutes
Cooking Time: 25-30 minutes
Number of Servings: 15 bars

Ingredients

- 1 cup cooked turkey, shredded (Lean protein)
- 1 cup rolled oats (Source of fiber)
- 1/4 cup dried cranberries (Antioxidant-rich)
- 1/4 cup sweet potato, mashed (Adds natural sweetness)
- 1 egg (Protein source)
- 1 tablespoon parsley, chopped (Adds flavor and nutrients)
- 1 tablespoon olive oil (Healthy fat)
- 1/4 cup water

Instructions

- Preheat your oven to 350°F (175°C) and grease a baking dish.
- In a large bowl, combine shredded turkey, rolled oats, dried cranberries, sweet potato, egg, chopped parsley, olive oil, and water.
- Mix the ingredients until well combined.
- Transfer the mixture to the greased baking dish and spread it out evenly.
- Bake in the preheated oven for 25-30 minutes, or until the bars are firm and lightly browned.
- Allow the bars to cool completely before cutting them into individual servings.

3

PEANUT BUTTER & BLUEBERRY BLISS BITES

 Preparation Time: 20 minutes (plus 1 hour refrigeration)
Cooking Time: No cooking required
Number of Servings: About 20 bites

Ingredients

- 1 cup blueberries (fresh or frozen) (Rich in antioxidants)
- 1/2 cup natural peanut butter (Protein and healthy fat)
- 2 cups oat flour (Source of fiber)

Instructions

- In a food processor, blend the blueberries until smooth.
- In a mixing bowl, combine the blueberry puree, peanut butter, and oat flour.
- Mix until a dough forms.
- Roll small portions of the dough into bite-sized balls.
- Place the balls on a parchment-lined tray and refrigerate for about 1 hour to set.

4

BLUEBERRY AND BANANA PUP MUFFINS

Preparation Time: 15 minutes
Cooking Time: 20 minutes
Number of Servings: Varies

Ingredients

- 1 cup blueberries (fresh or frozen)
- 2 ripe bananas, mashed
- 2 cups whole wheat flour
- 1 egg
- 1/4 cup honey
- 1 teaspoon baking powder
- 1/2 cup plain yogurt

Nutritional Value:

- Blueberries: Antioxidants, vitamins C and K
- Bananas: Potassium, vitamins B6 and C
- Whole wheat flour: Fiber, protein, and various nutrients
- Egg: Protein, vitamins B12 and D
- Honey: Antioxidants, natural sweetener
- Yogurt: Probiotics, calcium

Instructions

- Preheat your oven to 350°F (175°C) and line a muffin tin with paper liners.
- In a food processor, blend the blueberries until smooth.
- In a mixing bowl, combine the blueberry puree, mashed bananas, egg, honey, and yogurt. Mix well.
- In a separate bowl, whisk together the whole wheat flour and baking powder.
- Gradually add the dry ingredients to the wet ingredients, stirring until just combined.
- Spoon the batter into the prepared muffin tin, filling each cup about 2/3 full.
- Bake in the preheated oven for 20 minutes or until a toothpick inserted into the center comes out clean.
- Allow the muffins to cool completely before serving.

5

BEEF AND PUMPKIN PAW PRINT COOKIES

Preparation Time: 15 minutes
Cooking Time: 20 minutes
Number of Servings: About 20 cookies

Ingredients

- 1 cup cooked ground beef
- 1/2 cup canned pumpkin puree
- 2 cups whole wheat flour
- 1 egg

Instructions

- Preheat your oven to 350°F (175°C) and line a baking sheet with parchment paper.
- In a mixing bowl, combine the cooked ground beef, pumpkin puree, whole wheat flour, and the egg.
- Mix well until the ingredients form a dough-like consistency.
- Roll out the dough on a lightly floured surface to about 1/4-inch thickness.
- Use a paw-shaped cookie cutter to cut out adorable paw print shapes.
- Place the paw print cookies on the prepared baking sheet.
- Bake for 20 minutes or until the cookies are golden brown and firm.
- Allow the cookies to cool completely before serving.

CHICKEN AND BERRY BISCUIT DELIGHTS

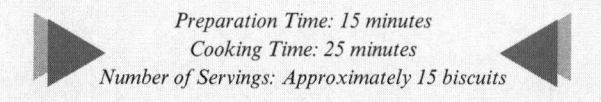

▶ Preparation Time: 15 minutes
Cooking Time: 25 minutes
Number of Servings: Approximately 15 biscuits ◀

Ingredients
- 1 cup cooked and shredded chicken
- 1/2 cup mixed berries (blueberries, strawberries, or raspberries)
- 2 cups oat flour
- 1 egg

Instructions
- Preheat your oven to 350°F (175°C) and line a baking sheet with parchment paper.
- In a bowl, combine the shredded chicken, mixed berries, oat flour, and the egg.
- Mix thoroughly until the ingredients come together in a dough.
- Roll the dough out on a floured surface to about 1/4-inch thickness.
- Use a biscuit cutter to create biscuit shapes and place them on the prepared baking sheet.
- Bake for 25 minutes or until the biscuits are golden brown.
- Allow the biscuits to cool before serving

7
TURKEY AND VEGGIE MUFFINS

Preparation Time: 20 minutes
Cooking Time: 30 minutes
Number of Servings: Makes 12 muffins

Ingredients
- 1 cup ground turkey
- 1/2 cup finely chopped mixed vegetables (carrots, peas, and green beans)
- 1 cup whole wheat flour
- 1 egg
- 1/4 cup unsweetened applesauce

Instructions
- Preheat your oven to 375°F (190°C) and line a muffin tin with paper liners.
- In a skillet over medium heat, cook the ground turkey until fully browned. Drain any excess fat.
- In a bowl, combine the cooked turkey, chopped vegetables, whole wheat flour, egg, and applesauce.
- Mix until all ingredients are well incorporated into a batter.
- Spoon the batter into the muffin tin, filling each cup about two-thirds full.
- Bake for approximately 30 minutes or until a toothpick inserted into the center comes out clean.
- Allow the muffins to cool before serving

8

CHEESY BACON BISCUIT BITES

Preparation Time: 15 minutes
Cooking Time: 20 minutes
Number of Servings: Makes 18 biscuit bites

Ingredients

- 1 cup shredded cheddar cheese
- 1/4 cup cooked and crumbled bacon
- 1 1/2 cups oat flour
- 1 egg
- 1/4 cup plain Greek yogurt

Instructions

- Preheat your oven to 350°F (175°C) and line a baking sheet with parchment paper.
- In a bowl, combine shredded cheddar cheese, crumbled bacon, oat flour, egg, and Greek yogurt.
- Mix until a dough forms, and then knead it lightly to ensure all ingredients are evenly distributed.
- Roll small portions of the dough into bite-sized balls and place them on the prepared baking sheet.
- Flatten each ball slightly with the back of a fork.
- Bake for approximately 20 minutes or until the edges are golden brown.
- Allow the cheesy bacon biscuit bites to cool before sharing.

TURKEY AND SWEET POTATO SLICES

Preparation Time: 10 minutes
Cooking Time: 25 minutes
Number of Servings: Makes 20 slices

Ingredients

- 1 cup ground turkey
- 1 cup mashed sweet potatoes
- 2 cups brown rice flour
- 1 egg
- 1 tablespoon coconut oil

Instructions

- Preheat your oven to 350°F (175°C) and grease a baking sheet.
- In a bowl, mix ground turkey, mashed sweet potatoes, brown rice flour, egg, and coconut oil until well combined.
- Roll the mixture into a dough and then flatten it on the baking sheet.
- Use a knife or cookie cutter to create individual slices.
- Bake for approximately 25 minutes or until the slices are firm and golden.
- Let the turkey and sweet potato slices cool completely before serving.

Chapter Three

FROZEN AND FROSTY TREATS FOR COOLING AND REFRESHING SNACKS

Contain in this chapter are recipes that are frozen in ice cube trays or molds and have a refreshing or cooling effect. These are great for hot summer days, soothing your dog's gums, or adding some variety to their diet.

1

BLUEBERRY AND YOGURT FROZEN POPS

Preparation Time: 10 minutes
Cooking Time: Freeze for 3 hours
Number of Servings: Varies

Ingredients
- 1 cup blueberries (fresh or frozen) (Rich in antioxidants, vitamins C and K.)
- 1 cup plain yogurt (Good source of protein, calcium, and probiotics)
- 1 tablespoon honey (Natural sweetener,)

Instructions
- In a blender, combine blueberries, plain yogurt, and honey
- Blend until smooth.
- Pour the mixture into popsicle molds.
- Freeze for at least 3 hours or until fully set.
- Once frozen, remove from molds and serve.

2

APPLE AND BANANA FROSTY BITES

Preparation Time: 15 minutes
Cooking Time: Freeze for 4 hours
Number of Servings: Varies

Ingredients

- 1 apple, diced.
  Nutritional Value: High in fiber, vitamins, and antioxidants.
- 1 banana, mashed.
  Nutritional Value: Good source of potassium, vitamin B6.
- 1/2 cup plain yogurt
  Nutritional Value: Provides protein, calcium, and probiotics.

Instructions

- In a bowl, mix diced apple, mashed banana, and plain yogurt.
- Spoon the mixture into bite-sized molds or an ice cube tray.
- Freeze for at least 4 hours or until solid.
- Once frozen, pop out the bites and serve.

3

TUNA AND PUMPKIN PAW-SICLES

Preparation Time: 15 minutes
Cooking Time: Freeze for 2 hours
Number of Servings: Varies

Ingredients

- 1 can tuna in water, drained
- 1/2 cup canned pumpkin
- 1 tablespoon plain yogurt
- 1 tablespoon honey

Nutritional value

- Tuna: Rich in protein and omega-3 fatty acids.
- Pumpkin: High in fiber, vitamins, and minerals.
- Yogurt: Provides probiotics and calcium.
- Honey: Natural sweetener with antioxidants.

Instructions

- In a bowl, mix the drained tuna, canned pumpkin, plain yogurt, and honey until well combined.
- Spoon the mixture into small silicone molds or ice cube trays.
- Freeze for about 2 hours or until the bites are firm.
- Pop the frozen treats out of the molds and store in an airtight container in the freezer

4

CHICKEN LIVER DELIGHTS

Preparation Time: 15 minutes
Cooking Time: Bake for 20 minutes
Number of Servings: Varies

Ingredients

- Cooked chicken liver (High in protein and vitamins)
- Blueberries (Rich in antioxidants)
- Eggs (Good source of protein)

Instructions

- Preheat the oven to 350°F (180°C).
- In a food processor, blend the cooked chicken liver and blueberries until well combined.
- Beat the eggs and add them to the liver-blueberry mixture. Blend until a dough forms.
- Scoop small portions of the dough onto a parchment-lined baking sheet.
- Bake for 20 minutes or until the treats are firm.
- Allow the treats to cool before serving
- Adjust portions based on your dog's size

5

SWEET POTATO AND TURKEY WRAPS

Preparation Time: 25 minutes
Cooking Time: Bake for 15 minutes
Number of Servings: About 12 wraps

Ingredients

- 2 cups cooked and mashed sweet potatoes (Rich in vitamins and fiber)
- 1 cup ground turkey (Lean protein)
- 1/2 cup carrots, grated (Provides additional nutrients)
- 1 cup whole wheat flour
- 1 egg (Good source of protein)

Instructions

- Preheat the oven to 375°F (190°C).
- In a large bowl, mix the mashed sweet potatoes, ground turkey, grated carrots, whole wheat flour, and egg.
- Knead the mixture until it forms a dough.
- Roll out the dough on a floured surface and cut it into small rectangles
- Place a small amount of the mixture onto each rectangle and roll it up.
- Arrange the wraps on a baking sheet and bake for 15 minutes or until golden brown.
- Allow the wraps to cool before serving.
- Ensure the wraps are suitable for your dog's size.

Chapter Four

NO-BAKE AND EASY TREATS FOR QUICK AND SIMPLE SNACKS

The recipes in this chapter do not require any baking or cooking and are quick and easy to make. These are great for busy owners, last-minute treats, or when you run out of ingredients.

1

CHICKEN AND CHEDDAR CHEW STICKS

▶ *Preparation Time: 15 minutes*
Cooking Time: Bake for 20 minutes
Number of Servings: About 15 sticks ◀

Ingredients
- 1 cup cooked chicken, shredded (Lean protein)
- 1 cup cheddar cheese, grated (Calcium and protein)
- 2 cups whole wheat flour
- 1 egg (Good source of protein)

Instructions
- Preheat the oven to 350°F (175°C).
- In a mixing bowl, combine the shredded cooked chicken, grated cheddar cheese, whole wheat flour, and egg.
- Mix the ingredients until a dough forms.
- Roll out the dough on a floured surface and cut it into stick shapes.
- Place the sticks on a parchment-lined baking sheet.
- Bake for about 20 minutes or until the sticks are golden brown.
- Allow the chew sticks to cool before serving.
- Ensure the chew sticks are an appropriate size for your dog and monitor them while enjoying this treat.

2

APPLE AND CARROT PUPCAKES

Preparation Time: 20 minutes
Cooking Time: Bake for 15 minutes
Number of Servings: Varies

Ingredients

- Diced apples (Rich in fiber and antioxidants)
- Shredded carrots (Excellent source of vitamins and minerals)
- Eggs (High-quality protein)

Instructions

- Preheat the oven to 350°F (175°C).
- In a bowl, mix the diced apples, shredded carrots, and eggs.
- Stir until the ingredients are well combined.
- Spoon the mixture into cupcake liners or a greased cupcake tin.
- Bake for approximately 15 minutes or until a toothpick inserted comes out clean.
- Allow the pupcakes to cool before serving.

PUMPKIN OAT COOKIES

Preparation Time: 10 minutes
Cooking Time: Bake for 12 minutes
Number of Servings: Varies

Ingredients

- Pumpkin puree (Rich in fiber and vitamins)
- Oats (Source of fiber and nutrients)
- Eggs (High-quality protein)

Instructions

- Preheat the oven to 350°F (175°C).
- In a bowl, combine the pumpkin puree, oats, and eggs.
- Mix the ingredients until a dough forms.
- Drop spoonfuls of the dough onto a parchment-lined baking sheet.
- Flatten each cookie slightly with the back of the spoon.
- Bake for approximately 12 minutes or until the edges are golden brown.
- Allow the cookies to cool completely before serving.

4

LIVER NIBBLES

Preparation Time: Varies
Cooking Time: 30-40 minutes
Number of Servings: Approximately 50

Ingredients

- 1 cup rolled oats(High in fiber)
- 1 cup all-purpose flour(carbohydrate)
- ½ pound chicken livers, rinsed and trimmed(Rich in protein and iron)
- 2 large eggs (source of protein)
- 1 tablespoon vegetable oil, or more as needed(Adds healthy fats)

Instructions

- Preheat the oven to 325 degrees F (165 degrees C). Grease a 9-inch square baking dish and line it with parchment paper.
- Add oats to the bowl of a food processor; pulse until finely chopped, 10 to 15 seconds. Transfer oats to a large bowl and mix in flour.
- Place livers in the food processor and process until smooth, 10 to 15 seconds. Add eggs and blend until well combined, about 10 seconds. Add oil and process until incorporated.
- Add liver mixture to oat and flour mixture; stir until well blended. Spoon into the prepared baking dish.
- Bake in the preheated oven until firm to the touch but not hard and crispy, 30 to 40 minutes.
- Remove from the oven and let cool completely before cutting into 50 pieces.

5

COCONUT AND BERRY BLISS BARS

Preparation Time: 15 minutes
Chilling Time: Refrigerate for 3 hours
Number of Servings: Varies

Ingredients

- 1 cup mixed berries (blueberries, strawberries, raspberries) (Rich in antioxidants)
- 1/2 cup coconut oil, melted (Healthy fats)
- 2 cups shredded coconut (Source of fiber)

Instructions

- In a mixing bowl, combine the mixed berries and melted coconut oil.
- Gradually mix in the shredded coconut until well combined.
- Line a baking dish with parchment paper and spread the mixture evenly.
- Refrigerate for at least 3 hours to set.
- Once set, cut into bars of your desired size.

6

BANANA AND PEANUT BUTTER SWIRLS

▶ Preparation Time: 10 minutes
Chilling Time: Refrigerate for 2 hours
Number of Servings: Varies ◀

Ingredients

- 2 ripe bananas, mashed (Potassium and natural sweetness)
- 1/2 cup natural peanut butter (Protein and healthy fats)

Instructions

- In a mixing bowl, combine the mashed bananas and natural peanut butter.
- Swirl the mixture until a smooth consistency is achieved.
- Line a tray with parchment paper and drop spoonfuls of the mixture.
- Use a toothpick to create swirl patterns on each bite.
- Refrigerate for at least 2 hours before serving.

7

PUMPKIN AND BLUEBERRY BITES

Preparation Time: 15 minutes
Chilling Time: Refrigerate for 3 hours
Number of Servings: Varies

Ingredients

- 1/2 cup pumpkin puree (Rich in vitamins)
- 1/2 cup blueberries (fresh or frozen) (Rich in antioxidants)
- 2 cups oat flour (Source of fiber)

Instructions

- In a mixing bowl, combine the pumpkin puree, blueberries, and oat flour.
- Mix until a dough forms.
- Shape small portions of the dough into bite-sized treats.
- Place the bites on a parchment-lined tray and refrigerate for at least 3 hours.
- Once chilled, the bites are ready.

8

OATMEAL AND APPLE ROUNDS

Preparation Time: 15 minutes
Chilling Time: Refrigerate for 1 hour
Number of Servings: Varies

Ingredients

- 1 cup rolled oats (Source of fiber)
- 1 apple, finely grated (Rich in vitamins and antioxidants)
- 1/2 cup plain yogurt (Protein and probiotics)

Instructions

- In a mixing bowl, combine the rolled oats, finely grated apple, and plain yogurt.
- Mix until a dough forms.
- Roll out the dough and use a cookie cutter to create round shapes.
- Place the rounds on a tray and refrigerate for at least 1 hour.
- Serve.

9

STRAWBERRY AND SWEET POTATO COOKIES

Preparation Time: 20 minutes
Baking Time: 15 minutes
Number of Servings: Varies

Ingredients

- 1 cup diced strawberries (Rich in vitamin C and antioxidants)
- 1 cup mashed sweet potato (High in fiber, vitamins, and minerals)
- 1 1/2 cups oat flour (Source of fiber)

Instructions

- Preheat the oven to 350°F (180°C) and line a baking sheet with parchment paper.
- In a mixing bowl, combine the diced strawberries, mashed sweet potato, and oat flour.
- Mix until a cookie dough forms.
- Drop spoonfuls of dough onto the prepared baking sheet.
- Bake for approximately 15 minutes or until the cookies are set.
- Let them cool before treating your pup.

10

CHEESY EGG BITES

▶ *Preparation Time: 10 minutes*
Cooking Time: Bake for 15 minutes
Number of Servings: Varies ◀

Ingredients

- 2 eggs
- 1/4 cup grated cheddar cheese
- 1/2 cup whole wheat flour

Nutritional Value:

- Eggs (Protein, Fatty Acids)
- Cheddar Cheese (Protein, Calcium)
- Whole Wheat Flour (Fiber)

Instructions

- Preheat the oven to 350°F (180°C).
- In a bowl, whisk the eggs.
- Add the grated cheddar cheese and whole wheat flour to the eggs. Mix until well combined.
- Spoon the mixture into a mini muffin tin or shape into bite-sized balls.
- Bake for 15 minutes or until golden brown.
- Allow the cheesy egg bites to cool before serving.

11

PUMPKIN AND EGG DELIGHTS

Preparation Time: 15 minutes
Cooking Time: Bake for 20 minutes
Number of Servings: Varies

Ingredients

- 1/2 cup canned pumpkin puree
- 1 egg
- 1 cup oat flour

Nutritional Value:

- Pumpkin (Fiber, Vitamins)
- Eggs (Protein, Fatty Acids)
- Oat Flour (Source of Fiber)

Instructions

- Preheat the oven to 350°F (180°C).
- In a bowl, mix the canned pumpkin puree, egg, and oat flour until a dough forms.
- Roll the dough into small balls or shape as desired.
- Place on a parchment-lined baking sheet and bake for 20 minutes or until firm.
- Cool the pumpkin and egg delights before serving.

12

BLUEBERRY EGG MUFFINS

▶ *Preparation Time: 12 minutes*
Cooking Time: Bake for 18 minutes
Number of Servings: Varies ◀

Ingredients

- 2 eggs
- 1/2 cup blueberries (fresh or frozen)
- 1 cup almond flour

Nutritional Value:

- Eggs (Protein, Fatty Acids)
- Blueberries (Antioxidants, Fiber)
- Almond Flour (Protein, Healthy Fats)

Instructions

- Preheat the oven to 350°F (180°C).
- In a bowl, whisk the eggs.
- Add blueberries and almond flour to the eggs. Mix until well combined.
- Spoon the mixture into muffin cups.
- Bake for 18 minutes or until a toothpick comes out clean.
- Allow the blueberry egg muffins to cool before serving.

Conclusion

We have thoroughly explored homemade dog treat recipes in this book, taking into account the difficulties busy people like you experience. We have learned that even when time isn't on our side, we can still provide our cherished furry pals delicious, nutritious treats. We have created recipes that promote ease of preparation and convenience without sacrificing flavor or quality.

We've made it simple for you to whip up these delicious snacks quickly by using readily available materials and offering straightforward directions. Each recipe shows the nutritional value of each ingredient and you get to know how to moderate the nutrition for your dogs. so you can be confident that it will provide results that will please both you and your furry friends.

Thank you for choosing *'Quick and Tasty Recipes for Busy Dog Parents.'* It was a joy crafting these recipes to bring delightful moments to your paw pals. If you have a moment, please consider leaving a positive feedback. Your input can help more dog parents discover these time-saving and delicious treats!

Printed in Great Britain
by Amazon